CONTENTS

Get Exploring

Over the course of a year, our gardens go through lots of changes. Autumn winds tug leaves from trees. Winter frosts make lawns sparkle. Spring pushes fresh shoots out of the soil. Summer fills flowerbeds with colour. Each season sparks stunning transformations and brings wildlife onto our doorsteps.

There's lots to do in the garden, whatever time of year it is. And while we look after our outside spaces, our outside spaces also look after us.

**The item should be returned or renewed
by the last date stamped below.**

Dylid dychwelyd neu adnewyddu'r eitem erbyn
y dyddiad olaf sydd wedi'i stampio isod.

Newport
CITY COUNCIL
CYNGOR DINAS
Casnewydd

2 2 AUG 2023

2 9 AUG 2023

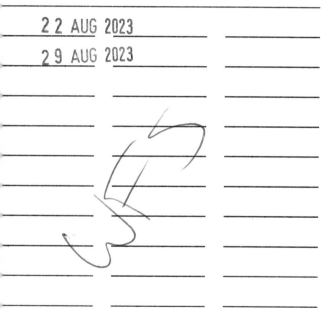

To renew visit / Adnewyddwch ar
www.newport.gov.uk/libraries

Exploring nature has been proven to help us feel calmer, less anxious and more relaxed. In this book, you can journey through the seasons, discovering things to spot, make, plant and do in the garden or outdoors all year round.

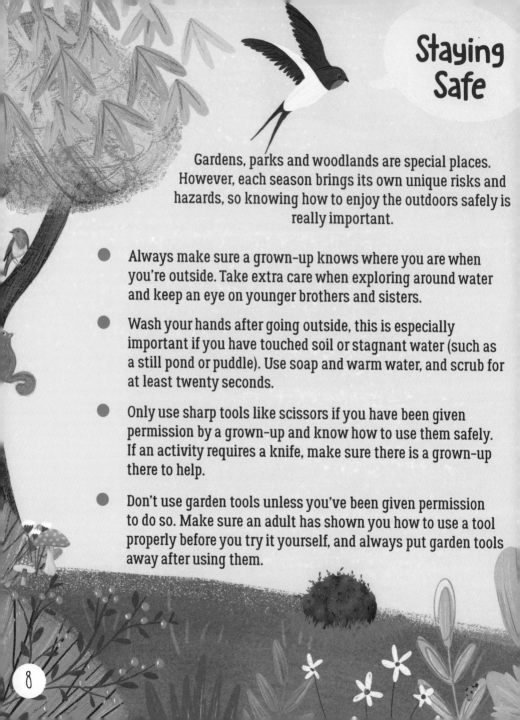

Staying Safe

Gardens, parks and woodlands are special places. However, each season brings its own unique risks and hazards, so knowing how to enjoy the outdoors safely is really important.

- Always make sure a grown-up knows where you are when you're outside. Take extra care when exploring around water and keep an eye on younger brothers and sisters.

- Wash your hands after going outside, this is especially important if you have touched soil or stagnant water (such as a still pond or puddle). Use soap and warm water, and scrub for at least twenty seconds.

- Only use sharp tools like scissors if you have been given permission by a grown-up and know how to use them safely. If an activity requires a knife, make sure there is a grown-up there to help.

- Don't use garden tools unless you've been given permission to do so. Make sure an adult has shown you how to use a tool properly before you try it yourself, and always put garden tools away after using them.

- Stay calm around stinging insects such as bees and wasps, and be aware that some hairy caterpillars can also cause skin irritation. Don't touch or swat at these creatures. Let a grown-up know if you get bitten or stung.

- Watch out for plants that prick or sting too, such as rose bushes, brambles and nettles.

- Never eat plants your find in the garden, or elsewhere outside, without permission from a grown-up you know and trust. Some poisonous plants, berries and mushrooms look incredibly similar to edible ones.

Safe in every season

- Drink plenty of water, particularly if it's hot, even if you don't feel thirsty.

- Wear a sunhat and sun cream if it's sunny to avoid burning or getting heatstroke.

- Wrap up warm when it's cold. Wear a hat, scarf, gloves and waterproof shoes.

Look out for more safety tips throughout the book!

9

Autumn Signs

As autumn gets underway, leaves turn fiery colours and fall to the ground. Short chilly days slip into long cold nights. Many creatures stock up on food before winter, feasting on juicy grubs and insects or the last nuts and berries. Some then find a cosy place to hibernate through the coming winter months.

What should you look for when out and about in autumn?

1. Tree cones

Coniferous trees like fir and pine start dropping their cones in autumn, so keep a look out for them on walks.

2. Seeds and nuts falling

From conkers to acorns, sycamore keys to chestnuts, autumn is the season when most trees drop their seeds, so that new trees can grow in springtime. Find out which seeds fall from which trees on pages 16–17.

3. Summer visitors leaving

Swifts, swallows and house martins are among
the birds that migrate south for the colder
months in late summer and early autumn.

4. Winter visitors arriving

Species to look and listen out for include redwings,
which you might hear calling overhead as they
migrate on November nights, and fieldfare.

Fieldfare

Redwing

These winter thrushes travel over
from Northern Europe and will be
on the hunt for something to eat
after their long journey, so look for
them in trees and bushes bursting
with berries.

11

Autumn Signs

5. Leaf transformations

Chlorophyll is the chemical inside leaves which makes them green. It turns sunlight into energy, through a process called photosynthesis. In autumn, trees prepare for winter by breaking down the chlorophyll in their leaves and sending the nutrients to their roots to be stored until it warms up again.

6. Animals hoarding food

Keep an eye out for squirrels and jays collecting acorns, a favourite food of both species. Animals that don't hibernate must still prepare for winter by eating lots to build up fat, or by storing food.

As the chlorophyll breaks down, the leaves lose their green colour, revealing red, yellow or orange, before falling to the ground.

7. Spiders spinning webs

Autumn is known as 'spider season', as suddenly these eight-legged creatures and their dew-filled webs seem to be everywhere! The spiders appearing in our homes haven't come in to shelter from the cold, however. They've actually always been here, hidden away, and are just more visible in autumn as they scurry around seeking mates.

Fungi growing

shrooms and toadstools are neither plants nor animals, but the fruiting bodies of ng fungi many of which feed on damp decaying matter, making autumn the perfect time them to pop up. Some common species to look out for (particularly in woodlands, though u may spot some in your garden) include:

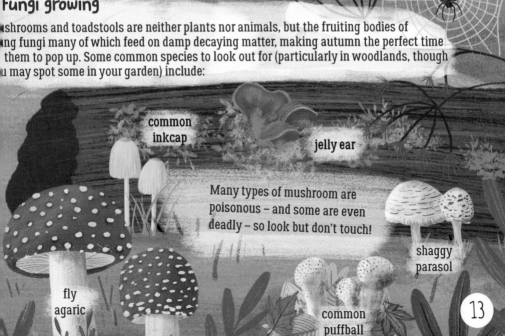

common inkcap

jelly ear

Many types of mushroom are poisonous – and some are even deadly – so look but don't touch!

shaggy parasol

fly agaric

common puffball

13

In the Autumn Garden

Here are four useful tasks you can carry out in the garden in autumn.

Build a compost bin

As plants start to die back and leaves begin to fall, autumn is the perfect time to build a simple compost bin. You can find lots of brilliant guides online, including instructions for building a special leaf mould compost bin on the RHS website.

Clear up fallen leaves

Rake up leaves from the lawn to stop them spoiling the grass, though it doesn't hurt to leave a few for the worms. Rather than burning them or throwing them away, let the leaves decay in your compost bin, so they can help new plants grow in years to come.

Pick ripe fruit

If you have fruit trees or bushes in your garden, autumn is often the best time to harvest apples, pears and plums, or pick blackberries. Fruit is ripe when it is firm and swollen, and can be pulled easily from the branch. Make sure you have permission from a grown-up before you pick or eat any fruit and wash it well first.

Plant spring bulbs

Autumn is the best time for planting spring bulbs such as daffodils, tulips and crocuses. Make sure the tips of the bulb are pointing up, and add a plant marker nearby, so you don't forget what you have planted! Find out more on pages 20–21.

Seed Spotting

Discover which seed or nut is produced by which tree with this spotter's guide.

Chestnut

Conker

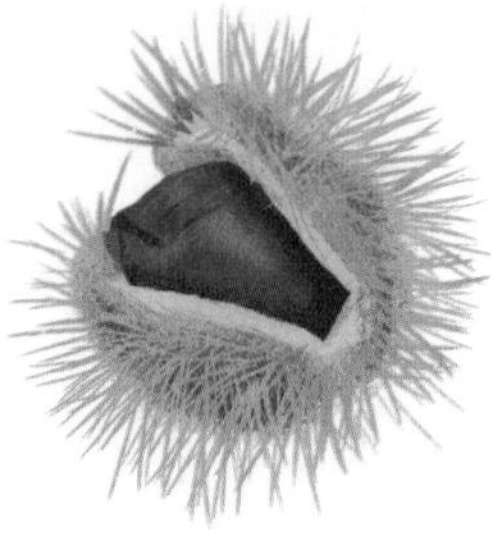

Acorn

Horse chestnut

Sweet chestnut

Oak

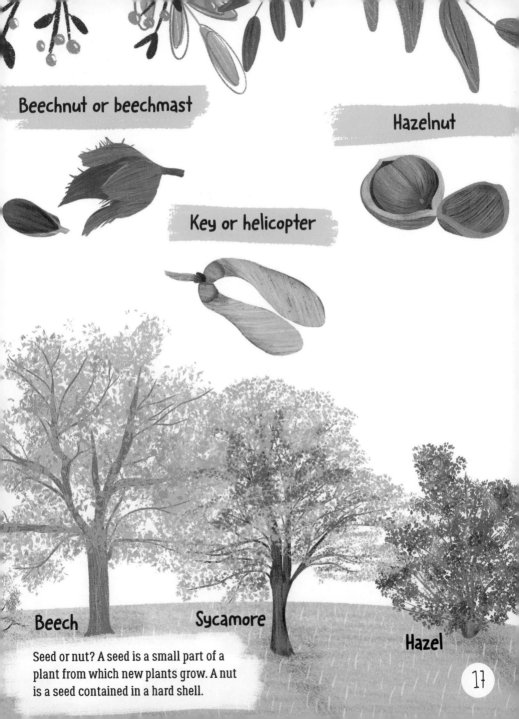

Beechnut or beechmast

Hazelnut

Key or helicopter

Beech

Sycamore

Hazel

Seed or nut? A seed is a small part of a plant from which new plants grow. A nut is a seed contained in a hard shell.

Bat Detective

Early autumn is a brilliant time to spot bats, when the weather is still fairly mild. Different species appear at different times, with some bats setting out to catch insects at sunset, and others hunting much later at night.

Brown long-eared bat

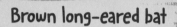

Found all over the UK. These bats have ears that are almost as long as their bodies. Their ears are held upright in flight, but curled back when at rest.

Daubenton's bat

Found all over the UK. You're most likely to spot these bats near water, as they catch insects flitting above rivers, lakes and ponds.

Each species of bat calls at a slightly different frequency, making it possible to tell them apart. Scientists use bat detectors – electronic devices that can hear the high-pitched noises bats make – to identify them.

Serotine bat

Found in south England and south Wales. Serotine bats can sometime be spotted near lampposts as they swoop to catch moths attracted to the light.

Common pipistrelle bat

Found all over the UK. Regular garden visitors, these teeny bats weigh around the same as a pound coin.

Soprano pipistrelle bat

Found all over the UK. Even smaller than common pipistrelles, soprano pipistrelles can still eat up to 3,000 insects a night.

Noctule bat

Found mostly in England and Wales, with fewer numbers in Scotland. Noctule bats fly above the treetops of their woodland homes, dipping down to catch insects on the wing. The UK's largest bat species, noctules have a wingspan up to 50cm.

Towards the end of autumn, bats settle in roosts to hibernate through the winter months. In the UK, all bat species and their roosts are protected, so it is illegal to harm a bat or damage a roost site.

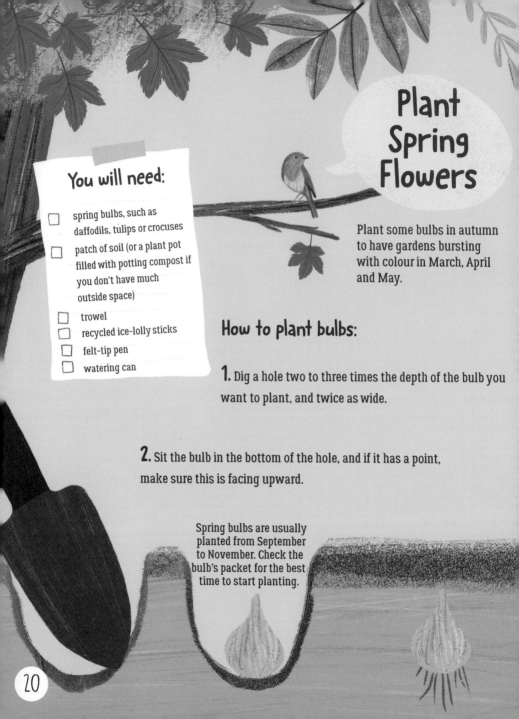

Plant Spring Flowers

You will need:

- [ ] spring bulbs, such as daffodils, tulips or crocuses
- [ ] patch of soil (or a plant pot filled with potting compost if you don't have much outside space)
- [ ] trowel
- [ ] recycled ice-lolly sticks
- [ ] felt-tip pen
- [ ] watering can

Plant some bulbs in autumn to have gardens bursting with colour in March, April and May.

How to plant bulbs:

1. Dig a hole two to three times the depth of the bulb you want to plant, and twice as wide.

2. Sit the bulb in the bottom of the hole, and if it has a point, make sure this is facing upward.

Spring bulbs are usually planted from September to November. Check the bulb's packet for the best time to start planting.

Always ask an adult for help when gardening. Remember, you'll also need their permission first.

3. Replace the soil around the bulb and pat it down gently. Careful not to tread on the area, or you might damage the bulb!

4. Write the name of the flower on a recycled ice-lolly stick and push it into the soil nearby, so you don't forget what's planted there.

5. Give the soil or compost a sprinkle of water, unless it is already moist.

6. Wait for your flowers to bloom in spring!

21

Bug Safari

Our gardens are bursting with life, and the more you look, the more you'll find.

Spot aphids and ladybirds on shoot tips and leaves. Aphids are small green, yellow, red or black insects that feed on plants. Ladybirds eat aphids, making them a gardener's friend! As autumn transitions into winter, many species of ladybird find somewhere out of the wind to shelter, such as in the cracks of tree bark or among dead plant stems.

Look for earthworms wriggling in the soil. Using tiny hooks on their bodies, worms drag leaves below the earth where they eat them. They break down organic matter, such as leaves and grass, into waste that plants can use. When they eat, they leave behind casts that are a very valuable type of fertilizer.

Find bees and butterflies on blooming flowers. As autumn goes on, you'll spot fewer pollinators in your garden. But some species, such as the red admiral butterfly or common carder bumblebee, can still be seen flitting from flower to flower late into the season.

Look under stones or rotten wood to reveal woodlice and millipedes. These many-legged creatures like dark, damp conditions. Woodlice and millipedes aren't closely related – woodlice are actually crustaceans, so have more in common with the crabs and shrimp you might spot at the seaside than with millipedes.

Can you see if there are any flowers in your garden that bees and butterflies are especially attracted to? Maybe buddleja, also known as butterfly bush, or fuchsias.

Grow a Pumpkin Patch

To harvest pumpkins in autumn, you'll need to plant them in spring. Check your pumpkin seed packet to make sure, but April or early May is usually the best time to sow the seeds indoors.

You will need:

- [ ] plant pot or recycled plastic container, such as a yoghurt pot with holes poked in the bottom for drainage
- [ ] potting compost
- [ ] pumpkin seeds (pick either decorative pumpkins, which are good for carving, or edible pumpkins, which can be cooked in pies and soups)
- [ ] patch of soil
- [ ] watering can

Pick your pumpkins in the autumn. It's best to harvest them a few days before you want to use them, then let them sit out in the sun to harden their skins and dry off their stalks.

How to grow pumpkins:

1. Fill your plant pot or plastic container with compost. Make a hole with your finger, around 2cm deep.

2. Place a pumpkin seed on its side in the hole and cover with compost. Put in a warm room.

3. Once your seed has sprouted, place on a sunny windowsill.

4. At the end of May, stand your pot outside in the day but take it in at night. In early June, find a patch of soil in your garden and use a trowel to make a hole twice as wide as your plant pot.

5. Gently tip your seedling out of the pot. Put it in the hole and add compost around it.

6. Give your pumpkin plants water whenever the soil feels dry and watch out for pests such as slugs and snails!

Make Nature Bunting

Bring the great outdoors indoors with this autumnal nature craft.
Hang up some nature bunting and enjoy the colours of autumn!

You will need:

- lots of autumn leaves (Try to pick clean, dry, complete leaves and see if you can find a mix of orange, red, yellow and brown ones. Avoid picking up leaves from muddy puddles or from fields where animals graze.)
- string
- scissors
- hairspray (optional)

1. Lay your leaves in a line on the floor, spaced evenly apart, with all the stalks pointing up.

2. Snip your string so it is about 40cm longer tha your line of leaves.

3. Starting 20cm from the end of your piece of string, tie it around the first stalk.

4. Continue tying the string around each of the stalks, keeping the leaves evenly spaced, until all the leaves are attached.

5. If you'd like your bunting to last longer, spray each leaf with a bit of hairspray.

Remember
to wash your
hands with
soap and water
after this
activity.

Ask a grown-up
for help when
using scissors.

Bake an Apple Crumble

Fruit tastes best when it's fresh, so you could see if your neighbours, or a local community garden, have any apple trees that you could pick fruit from for this yummy crumble.

You will need:

- [ ] 120g plain flour
- [ ] 80g caster sugar
- [ ] 90g unsalted butter
- [ ] 400g eating apples
- [ ] A pinch of cinnamon (optional)

Make sure a grown-up is always on hand to help you with this activity, particularly when using a knife or the oven.

1. Heat the oven to 190°C / 170°C fan or gas mark 5. Weigh out 50g of caster sugar, then add it to a bowl with the flour and mix.

2. Cut 60g of butter into small cubes. Use your fingertips to rub it into the flour and sugar, until the mixture looks like breadcrumbs.

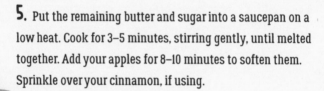

3. To make your topping extra crunchy, spread the crumble topping evenly across a baking tray and put it in the oven for 8–10 minutes. It should have a light gold colour.

4. While the crumble topping is in the oven, peel the apples using a vegetable peeler. Chop them in half, then cut out the core, before chopping the rest of the fruit into bite-size pieces.

5. Put the remaining butter and sugar into a saucepan on a low heat. Cook for 3–5 minutes, stirring gently, until melted together. Add your apples for 8–10 minutes to soften them. Sprinkle over your cinnamon, if using.

6. Spoon the fruit into an ovenproof dish, then top with the crumble mixture. Cook for 15 minutes, until golden and starting to bubble.

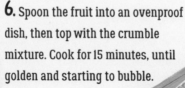

Winter Signs

In winter, cold breezes make bare branches shiver. Silver frost trails across the garden. Beneath the ground, or deep in log piles or tree hollows, many creatures snooze through the dark, freezing months.

What should you look for when out and about in winter?

1. Tracks in the snow

Wildlife might be harder to spot in winter, but signs of garden visitors are still readily found. Look out for these tracks across your lawn, or in a local park or woodland – they'll be easiest to spot after it has snowed!

2. Insects hunkering down

You'll spot fewer creepy crawlies in your garden as the frosts draw in, but many minibeasts can still be discovered deep in leaf piles, where the air is a little warmer.

3. Ladybird huddles

Some ladybird species overwinter alone, but others seek out places to spend the winter together in huddles of dozens of insects.

Don't pick berries unless you're with a grown-up who knows what they're looking for. Some wild berries are toxic and can make you really ill.

4. Ripe berries

Fruits and berries appear on many different trees and plants in the autumn, helping wildlife to survive the winter. Look out for deep purple sloes on blackthorn, bright red clusters of berries on holly bushes and orange-red hips on dog roses.

31

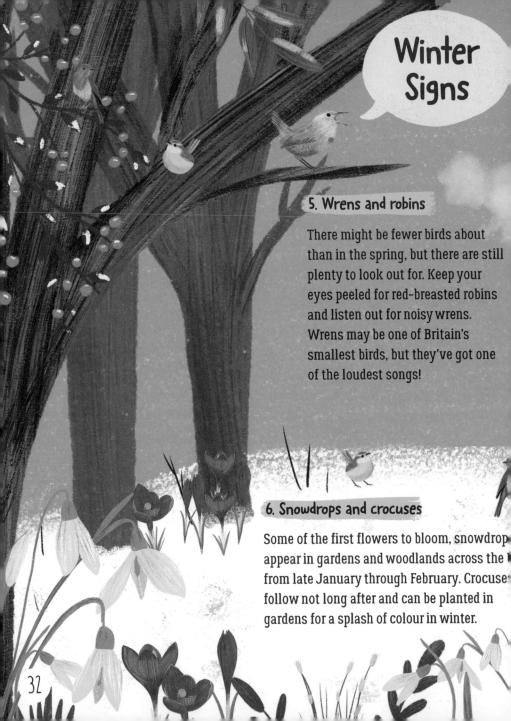

Winter Signs

5. Wrens and robins

There might be fewer birds about than in the spring, but there are still plenty to look out for. Keep your eyes peeled for red-breasted robins and listen out for noisy wrens. Wrens may be one of Britain's smallest birds, but they've got one of the loudest songs!

6. Snowdrops and crocuses

Some of the first flowers to bloom, snowdrop appear in gardens and woodlands across the from late January through February. Crocuse follow not long after and can be planted in gardens for a splash of colour in winter.

7. Bare trees

Deciduous trees can appear brown and bare in the winter, but if you look closely, you might discover colourful lichens and mosses clinging to the bark.

8. Flocks of starlings

Look up at dusk for your best chance of spotting a vast flock of starlings sweeping across the sky, known as a murmuration. The birds gather above roosting sites, before settling down for the night.

In the Winter Garden

Here are four useful tasks you can carry out in the garden in winter.

Look after birds

If you have a bird bath, check it hasn't frozen over and replace the water regularly. Consider putting out a bird feeder, too, to help birds get enough to eat when insects and berries are scarce. Get help with cleaning this out regularly. If you have a bird box, winter is a good time to clean it out, ready for spring visitors.

Protect plants from frost

Small pot plants can be brought inside, and larger plants protected by putting a layer of straw around the heart of the plant, or covering it with a sack and securing with twine.

Shake snow off branches

Snowy trees are lovely to look at, but if a branch becomes too heavily laden with snow, it might snap off! Ask a grown-up to help you brush or shake the snow away especially on evergreens and conifers after a heavy flurry.

Clean your garden tools

Make sure your spade, trowel and secateurs are squeaky clean, ready for spring gardening. Keep your tools in a shed or other covered area, out of the cold and damp. Always ask a grown-up to help you when handling tools.

Wildlife in Winter

Wintertime can be tough for our garden wildlife. There's less food to eat, cold winds to battle with and the risk of heavy rain, or even snow.

The long sleep

Hibernation is one way that some warm-blooded animals deal with the harsh conditions of winter. When animals hibernate, they find somewhere safe to curl up. Their body temperature drops, they don't eat and they hardly even breathe. In the UK, hibernators include dormice, bats and hedgehogs. Other animals such as reptiles also hunker down, often below ground.

The animal with one of the longest hibernations is the edible dormouse, introduced to Britain by the Romans. They can hibernate for up to eleven months!

If your pond freezes over, melt a hole at the edge in the surface using warm water, so that wildlife can get to the water for a drink as well as get in and out of the pond.

Forgotten frogs

Amphibians such as frogs, toads and newts don't hibernate, but they become much less active when the temperature drops. To stop their skin drying out, they have to find somewhere damp, such as a pile of leaves or a muddy burrow. Some frogs even overwinter at the bottom of ponds.

Winter bird watching

There's still plenty of wide-awake winter wildlife to look out for in your garden. Birds don't hibernate and often come to visit garden bird feeders. With no leaves on deciduous trees and bushes it's also easier to spot them than in summer.

Open Your Ears

See if you can spend fifteen minutes simply listening to nature's sounds. Hearing natural noises has been proven to help humans feel more relaxed!

Stand in a garden, forest or other green space. Close your eyes if you feel comfortable, or just focus on one point and let your mind wander.

See if you can count five nature sounds. Listen out for subtle differences – is one bird singing louder than another? Does the wind sound noisier through the branches of that tree, or this one?

What nature sounds can you hear?

Birds singing?

The grass swishing?

Rain falling?

Leaves being whisked by the wind?

The sound of running water, such as a stream or river, can also help to make us feel relaxed.

Build a Hibernation Home

Provide a cosy home for hibernating animals to snooze in through the winter months.

You will need:

- around 25 old bricks
- a large plastic tray
- dry leaves, hay or straw
- large stones or more bricks
- sticks, twigs and leaves
- some sand (optional)

How to make:

1. Find a flat, quiet and shady spot in your garden and lay the bricks out in the below shape. Make sure the entranc⟩ is facing west or south (to avoid chilly north winds!).

2. Add another layer of bricks in the same pattern, to build the walls higher.

3. Add a third layer, this time filling in the gaps, like this.

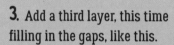

4. Add a final two bricks to create an entrance tunnel. This should stop any cats from getting too close to hibernating visitors.

5. Line the floor of your hibernation home with dry leaves, hay or straw. Put your plastic tray on top to create a roof. The tray should be a little wider and longer than your walls.

6. Use stones or more bricks to weigh down your tray. It's really important to make sure the roof will be sturdy and secure, whatever the weather. If the tray falls off, or falls into the home, it could expose or hurt your hibernator.

7. Cover your hibernation home with sticks, twigs and leaves to help camouflage it. It's now ready for guests!

8. Leave the home undisturbed until late spring. If you like, scatter some sand at the entrance and watch out for pawprints, to see if somebody has moved in!

If you live in the UK, the most likely visitor for your hibernation home is a hedgehog. Make sure hedgehogs can get in and out of your garden by digging a hole under your fence. If all your neighbours also do this, you can create a 'hedgehog highway' down your street!

You could also fill a plant pot with hay and put it on its side nearby. That way, if some of the hay disappears, you'll be able to tell if a hibernator is using the house!

Most hibernators start to settle down in late autumn, so set up your hibernation home at the end of the summer for the best chance of someone moving in.

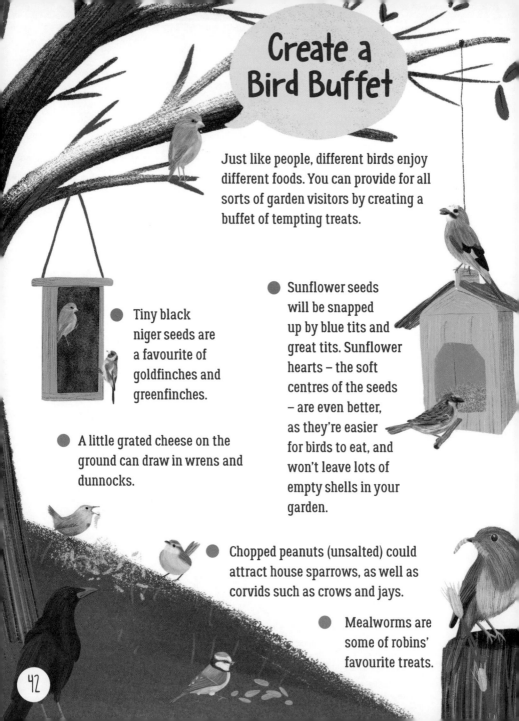

Create a Bird Buffet

Just like people, different birds enjoy different foods. You can provide for all sorts of garden visitors by creating a buffet of tempting treats.

● Tiny black niger seeds are a favourite of goldfinches and greenfinches.

● Sunflower seeds will be snapped up by blue tits and great tits. Sunflower hearts – the soft centres of the seeds – are even better, as they're easier for birds to eat, and won't leave lots of empty shells in your garden.

● A little grated cheese on the ground can draw in wrens and dunnocks.

● Chopped peanuts (unsalted) could attract house sparrows, as well as corvids such as crows and jays.

● Mealworms are some of robins' favourite treats.

Birds need fat in winter to keep warm. You can buy fat (suet) balls, or it's easy to make your own.

1. To make a vegetarian version, melt coconut oil in a pan until it becomes liquid.

2. Once it has cooled, stir in peanut butter (look for a brand without added salt or sugar, and without palm oil), bird seed and flour.

3. Mush together into firm ball shapes with your fingers. Dust with flour, so the ball isn't too oily, or it can damage birds' wings.

4. Use a wooden skewer to push a ribbon through and hang the ball from a branch.

Remember to ask a grown-up to help you when using the hob!

Make a Wildlife Wall

Insects like to slip into cracks and crevices, particularly in the cold winter months. Give them a cosy place to stay by creating a wildlife wall.

You will need:

- [ ] old bricks
- [ ] planks of old wood
- [ ] hollow bamboo canes, cut into short lengths
- [ ] hay, straw, moss and dead leaves

1. Pick a quiet, sheltered area of your garden for your wildlife wall.

You could check at your local refuse centre for suitable material. Don't worry if you can't get hold of many bricks as it doesn't matter how big or small you build your wall. Even a mini wall can make a good home for lots of creepy crawlies.

2. Start with a layer of bricks, leaving gaps between them. Turn engineering bricks with holes through the middle on their sides so the holes are visible. Lay a plank of wood on top.

3. Add another layer of bricks, then another plank of wood, and repeat until you run out. Remember to leave lots of gaps.

4. Stuff some of the gaps with the short bamboo canes, some with hay or straw, and some with moss or dead leaves.

See if you can spot signs of residents, maybe a few spiders webs or a flash of colour from a ladybird wingcase. Earwigs and delicate fairy-like lacewings might also shelter in there.

5. Try not to disturb your wildlife wall; its inhabitants will thrive best when left alone. However, you might need to top up the hay, moss and straw every now and again, as birds may pinch it for nesting material!

Make a twig star

This simple star made from sticks can make a lovely winter decoration, or even a festive gift for a friend or family member.

You will need:

- [ ] five twigs
- [ ] secateurs
- [ ] twine

1. Using your secateurs, snip your twigs to the same length.

2. Take two twigs and cross the top of one over the other, to form two sides of a triangle. Tie together tightly with twine, at the point the two twigs cross.

3. Repeat that step with two more twigs, so you have two two-sided twig triangles.

4. Tie a stick of one triangle to the opposite stick of the other, at a thirty-degree angle. Then cross the other two sticks over, to interlock the triangles.

5. Use twine to tie your final twig in place, completing your special star. Add a loop of twine at the top of your star to hang it!

Make a Winter Solstice Lantern

Brighten up dark winter nights with this special lantern.

To press your leaves and flowers, pick dry and clean ones in the summer or autumn and tuck between the pages of a book. Pile some other books on top, to add weight, then leave for a week. Keep them safe until you need them for a craft!

You will need:

- [ ] recycled jam jar, washed and dried
- [ ] liquid glue
- [ ] glue stick or paint brush
- [ ] pressed leaves and flowers
- [ ] electric tealight

How to make:

1. Paint the outside of your jar with PVA glue.

2. While the glue is still wet, stick on some pressed leaves and flowers. You can cover all the glass or leave some gaps.

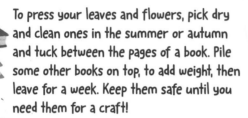

In the UK, winter solstice falls on the 21st December and is the shortest day of the year.

3. Wait for everything to dry, then paint another layer of glue over the leaves and flowers.

4. Once your lantern has dried, you can put your electric tealight inside and let it glow.

Spring Signs

In spring, tree branches blush with fragile blossom. New shoots push their way out of the soil. Birds gather twigs for their nests, before laying eggs that hatch into hungry chicks.

What should you look for when out and about in spring?

1. May flowers

Look out for blossoming hawthorn, also know as the May tree. It's easily confused with blackthorn, which also has pretty cream-coloured flowers. You can tell the difference between the two by looking at their leaves; blackthorn leaves are oval, whereas hawthorn leaves have jagged edges. Both have long sharp thorns so take care not to get pricked.

2. Birds building nests

You'll start to notice a lot more bird action from March onwards, and may even spot garden birds carrying twigs in their beaks for their nests. Later in spring, you might notice birds gathering grubs to feed their newly hatched chicks.

3. Noisy dawn choruses

This is one to listen out for, rather than look out for! On early mornings from April to June, birds are at their loudest as males try to win female mates with their song. To hear the first songster of the morning you'd need to be awake at around 4a.m.!

4. Buds appearing

You should be able to spot green shoots appearing on previously bare branches, as the sunlight hours grow longer. The fattest buds, especially on fruit trees, contain flowers as well as leaves.

5. Bluebells and other spring flowers

Bright bluebells and white ransoms (also called wild garlic as all parts smell of garlic when rubbed) carpet woodlands, while in gardens tulips, daffodils, primrose and other spring flowers bloom.

6. Migratory birds arriving

Tired travellers start to arrive in the UK in early spring, adding their voices to the morning chorus. Listen out for chiffchaffs (their 'chiff chaff, chiff chaff' song sounds like they're saying their own name!) and the unmistakeable, though increasingly rare, call of the cuckoo. Both have migrated all the way from Africa, where they spend the winter.

7. Frogs returning to ponds

After a winter of inactivity, warmer weather triggers the reappearance of amphibians. Frogs are usually the first to return to ponds, followed by toads and newts. Female frogs lay their spawn in ponds and, after a few weeks, tadpoles emerge and start to feed on algae.

8. Other creatures waking up

Just like amphibians, warming days means bats, hedgehogs, grass snakes and other animals also become active again. You'll also notice more minibeasts in the flowerbeds, as the whole garden starts coming back to life. Watch for the flash of lime-green or yellow wings of the brimstone butterfly and the large buzzing queen bumblebees seeking out flowers and new nest spots.

53

Prune shrubs

Ask a grown-up if there are any shrubs that want pruning at this time of year. Pruning means cutting back dead or overgrown bits of a plant, to encourage new, healthy growth. Using secateurs, cut old or dead wood from the base of the plant. Then, where stems are growing close together or crossing, cut one away to prevent them rubbing together. You can also reduce the height of the whole shrub by cutting stems on an angle, just above a bud. Make sure you check no birds are nesting in the plant before pruning it and remember to wear thick gloves especially if you're pruning a thorny plant such as a rose!

Here are four useful tasks you can carry out in the garden in spring.

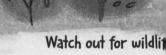

Watch out for wildlife

Waking hibernators will be thirsty so you could leave out a bowl of fresh clean water for them. Hungry hedgehogs will appreciate some meat-based (not fish-based) cat or dog food, or you can buy special hedgehog food at your local garden centre

You can tell which stems are dead if they are brown all the way through.

54

'No Mow May'

Most wildflowers bloom in May and are a vital source of nectar for bees and other pollinators. Ask your parents if they are happy to avoid mowing the lawn or a patch of it in May to let flowers such as daisies, dandelions and buttercups bloom.

Plant vegetables

Early spring is a good time to plant potatoes, leeks, carrots and broad beans, ready for a summer harvest. Wait until late spring to sow sweetcorn, courgettes, French and runner beans.

55

Discover Garden Birds

Look out for these visitors in spring!

Goldfinch

Great tit

Blue tit

Long-tailed tit

Long-tailed tits use moss, feathers, hay and wool to build their nests, along with spiderwebs to stick it together and to stick lichen to the outside. Because the stretchy spiderwebs are woven into the nest, it expands as the chicks grow.

Wood pigeon

Female chaffinch

Male chaffinch

Female blackbird

Male blackbird

You could help birds build their nests by draping wool, hay and twigs over branches for them to take away.

Wren

Wrens can sing 740 notes in one minute! Our ears aren't sensitive enough to hear them all, but birds' ears are.

Dunnock

Female house sparrow

Male house sparrow

Become a Leaf Detector

By the end of spring, the trees in gardens, parks and woodlands should be bushy with bright green leaves once again. But which tree is which?

Oak

Horse chestnut

Ash

Maple

Sycamore

Beech

Plane

Lime

Alder

All the above are deciduous trees, meaning they lose their leaves in the autumn and grow new ones in the spring.

Grow Your Own Runner Beans

Plant these crunchy green beans in late spring so they're ready to pick in summer.

You will need:

- [ ] small plant pots or recycled yoghurt pots, washed and dried, with holes poked through the bottom for drainage
- [ ] potting compost
- [ ] runner bean seeds
- [ ] a watering can
- [ ] some space in your garden, or bigger plant pots
- [ ] bamboo canes, around 1–1.5 m tall (ask a grown-up to push a cork on the end of each stick if they are sharp)
- [ ] trowel or small spade
- [ ] garden twine

Ask a grown-up for help when using secateurs or scissors.

How to grow:

1. Fill a few plant pots or yoghurt pots with compost. Press a runner bean seed into each one, so the seeds are about 5cm deep.

2. Sprinkle over some water so the soil is damp. Put your pots in a warm spot, such as on a windowsill, and wait for them to germinate.

3. Water the shoots regularly over the next couple of weeks. Once the danger of frosts is past, usually in late May or June, they are ready to move outside. Stand them for a few days in somewhere sheltered such as a greenhouse or covered porch, until they have adjusted to being outdoors.

planting in the ground, choose a
\[su\]nny spot, where the soil drains well
\[ch\]eck puddles don't appear there when
\[it r\]ains). Firmly push your bamboo
\[can\]es into the ground. You'll need one
\[can\]e per runner bean plant.

5. If growing in large pots on
a patio or balcony, fill your
bigger pots with compost.
You'll need one pot per runner
bean plant. Push a bamboo
cane into each pot.

\[U\]se a trowel or small spade to
\[dig\] a hole at the base of each
\[ba\]mboo cane.

7. Carefully transfer a runner bean
plant (and a handful of extra compost
if planting in the ground) into each
hole, push the soil or compost back
around the roots, and sprinkle over a
little water.

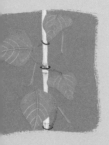

\[...\] Water the plants every few
\[da\]ys, and more regularly if
\[it's\] hot and dry, so the soil or
\[po\]tting compost is always a
\[lit\]tle damp.

9. As the runner beans
grow, use garden twine
to tie new shoots to the
canes, encouraging the
plants to grow up them.

10. Pick the beans when
they are between 15–20cm
long. This should be around
12 to 16 weeks after you
planted them.

Grow Your Own Strawberries

You can grow strawberries from seed, but it can take a long time for the fruit to appear. Some gardeners prefer to get a head start by planting a young strawberry plant.

The best time to start growing strawberries is during spring or summer because they need to grow in sun.

You will need:

☐ young strawberry plant (from garden centre)
☐ large plant pot
☐ pebbles or small stones
☐ potting compost
☐ watering can

If you plant a strawberry plant in the garden instead, it will grow long stems that run along the ground and bed themselves in the soil to make lots of new plants. These are called runners.

How to grow:

1. If your plant pot has one big drainage hole in the bottom, put a few pebbles or broken pieces of old pot over it to stop the compost washing out.

2. Fill your pot a half to two-thirds full with compost. Carefully transfer your strawberry plant into the plant pot, trying not to damage the roots. Add more compost to fill the pot, but be careful not to cover the top of your strawberry plant.

3. Put your plant outside in the sun and water it whenever the compost starts to look dry. Look out for the white flowers with yellow centres. When the strawberries start to grow from the centre of the flowers, they will be green, but soon they will turn completely red. When your strawberries are red, they are ripe and ready to eat.

Wildfulness Walk

Life is sometimes so busy that we spend a lot of time in our own heads! Taking a moment to notice the little things, such as how your body feels as you walk around a garden, can help bring you back to the here and now.

1. If you have a garden with a lawn, you could take your shoes and socks off, but make sure there's nothing sharp in your path first. If you don't have a garden, try walking in a local park or woodland but keep your shoes on.

2. Get in a comfortable position and stand still for a moment. What does the ground feel like beneath your feet?

3. Take a slow step forward, noticing how it feels to transfer your weight from one foot to the other. Think about the different sensations as you press your foot into the ground.

4. Continue walking around the garden or park, either in a circle, or weaving around. Notice how your body feels with each step. Does anything tingle?

5. Finish by standing still for a moment, taking in how each part of your body feels from your toes, all the way up to your head.

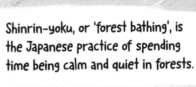

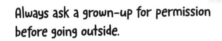

Always ask a grown-up for permission before going outside.

Shinrin-yoku, or 'forest bathing', is the Japanese practice of spending time being calm and quiet in forests.

Create a Spring Scrapbook

Spring is a time for new starts – making it the perfect time to begin a nature diary or scrapbook. Here are a few ideas to get you started.

You will need:

- ☐ notepad
- ☐ pen or pencil
- ☐ colouring pencils or fine liners
- ☐ glue stick
- ☐ camera (optional)

Take photos of any minibeasts you spot, then try to identify them using online resources. You could draw a quick sketch in your scrapbook and add labels.

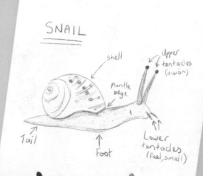

SNAIL

shell

Upper tentacles (vision)

Mantle edge

Tail

Foot

Lower tentacles (feel, smell)

Maple →

← Ash

Take small clippings of plants or fallen leaves and stick them into your journal. Remember to make sure you have permission from whoever owns the property before you pick any plants, and never pick flowers from parks or wildflowers from the countryside.

Male Chaffinch

9/2/21

Look out for birds, mammals, reptiles and amphibians and make notes about any interesting behaviour you see. You could try drawing a quick sketch from life, or making a more detailed drawing from a photograph.

Date each entry, so you start to build up a picture of the year. You'll see how, season by season, nature brings new delights and surprises.

Cook Spring Greens Pasta

Make sure a grown-up is always on hand to help you with this activity, particularly when using a knife or boiling water and using the hob.

You will need:

- [ ] 300g dried pasta (any kind of pasta will work!)
- [ ] 150g spring greens
- [ ] 200g fine beans
- [ ] 150g cream cheese
- [ ] 1 tablespoon pesto
- [ ] 1 tablespoon lemon juice
- [ ] 1 tablespoon chopped fresh chives
- [ ] 4 tablespoons grated hard cheese, such as Parmesan or a vegetarian alternative
- [ ] salt and pepper

Fresh greens are delicious in a creamy pasta. Discover how to make a tasty dinner for your friends and family. This recipe serves four people.

1. Cook the pasta in a pan of boiling water, according to the packet's instructions.

2. Wash the spring greens and green beans and pat dry with kitchen towel. Chop the spring greens into thin strips. Trim the ends off the fine beans.

3. When the pasta has 5 minutes cooking time left, add the vegetables to the boiling water.

4. Drain the pasta and greens, leaving just a little water at the bottom of the pan.

5. Stir through the cream cheese and pesto, until it has melted into a sauce. Add the lemon juice, chives and grated cheese. Finally, season with a little salt and pepper, then serve!

You could substitute the fine beans for homegrown runner beans on pages 60-61! Cut the tough ends off, then chop in half lengthways, trim into thin strips, then cook as above.

Summer Signs

In summer, garden flowers such as roses, geraniums and lilies open their petals as the sun shines down. Wings whirr as bees and butterflies follow a winding path from bloom to bloom. Fledglings, born in the spring, take their first flights.

What should you look for when out and about in summer?

1. Wildflowers blooming
As spring flowers fade, summer wildflowers such as poppies, honeysuckle and foxgloves come into bloom.

2. Bees and butterflies visiting flowers
The flowerbeds are a flurry of activity as bees and butterflies collect nectar. In the UK, the vast majority of bee species are solitary, meaning they live alone rather than in hives. Of all the 287 British bee species only one, the honeybee, makes honey.

3. Swifts, swallows and house martins on the wing

Having arrived from Africa in the spring, these screechy migrants spend the summer swooping above our rooftops on the hunt for insects to feed their young. All three species favour buildings as their nesting sites.
Here's how to tell the difference:

Swift
crescent shape
wings; high fliers;
dark feathers

Swallow
red throat; long
tail streamers

House martin
smaller than swifts
and swallows; forked
tail; white belly

4. Fledgling flights

Chicks born in spring will now have grown their flight feathers. They'll begin to take their first tentative flaps, before leaving their nests. Though you'd be very lucky to spot this in your garden, there are lots of brilliant live cameras online to explore.

Summer Signs

5. An abundance of insects

From grasshoppers chirping in the grass to damselflies hovering over ponds, six-legged creatures seem to be everywhere in summer! Insects' body temperatures change with the environment, so warm weather often triggers an increase in insect activity.

6. Darting dragonflies and damselflies

Look for these colourful predators darting over ponds, on the hunt for prey. To tell the difference between the two, look at their wings. Damselflies often have skinny, twig-like bodies, whereas dragonflies usually have broader or plumper bodies. When at rest, dragonflies keep their wings open like a plane and damselflies close them.

7. Green leaves

Trees should now be bursting with leaves, though in darker shades of green than the fresh shoots of spring. Some trees such as copper beech develop purple leaves. Flick back to pages 58–59 for help identifying leaves.

8. Bats zipping about

With young bats to raise back at their roosts, bats can often be spotted on warm summer nights, whizzing around, searching for tasty insects.

In the Summer Garden

Here are four useful tasks you can carry out in the garden in summer.

Pick weeds from flowerbeds

Pull up weeds (unwanted plants) from yo[ur] beds, giving your planted flowers the best chance to flourish, but leave them where [they] are doing no harm, such as in your lawn. [To] take out the whole root system, or the we[ed] will just grow again.

Top up your bird bath

Hot and thirsty birds will appreciate a bowl of cool, fresh water during the dry, sunny months. Some birds, such as house sparrows, take dust baths too, by rolling about in dust or soil as part of their preening process.

Watch for plant eaters

Keep an eye out for creatures such as slugs and aphids which might be nibbling on your plants and remove if necessary. You are more likely to spot slugs and snails after it has rained and in the evening when the sun has gone down. Remember many predators rely on these animals for food.

Water often

Your garden will need lots of water to thrive when it is hot and dry. It's best to use a watering can and water from a rainwater butt, rather than a hosepipe, which wastes valuable drinking water. Try to aim the water at the soil directly under your plant rather than over the leaves – after all, it is the roots that need the drink.

Summer is the best time to harvest veggies you planted in spring!

75

Butterflies and Moths

Discover ten common species of butterflies and moths that you might spot this summer.

Butterflies

Red admiral

Peacock butterfly

Orange tip

Common blue

Small tortoiseshell

Around the world, there are about ten times as many moth species as butterfly species. In the UK, we have around 60 species of butterfly and around 2,500 species of moth!

Moths

Cinnabar

Elephant hawkmoth

Swallowtail moth

Scalloped oak

Silver Y

Sadly, pollinators including moths and butterflies are declining worldwide. Planting more plants for pollinators will give them a much-needed energy boost during the hot summer months.

77

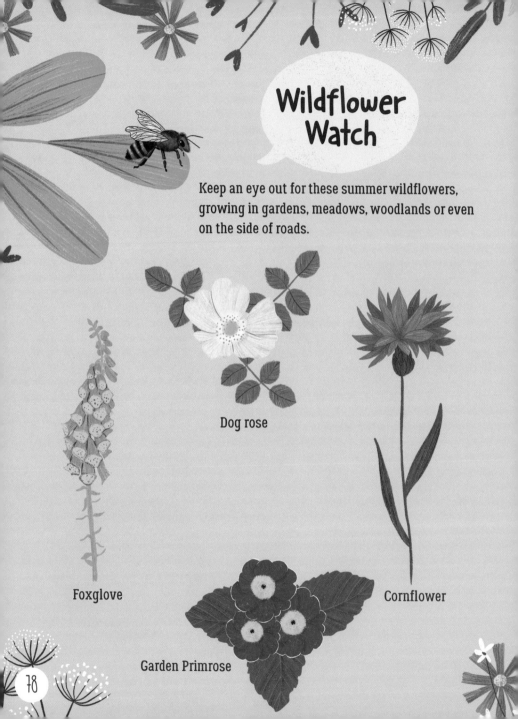

Wildflower Watch

Keep an eye out for these summer wildflowers, growing in gardens, meadows, woodlands or even on the side of roads.

Dog rose

Cornflower

Foxglove

Garden Primrose

Forget-me-not

Pyramid orchid

Honeysuckle

Oxeye daisy

Cow parsley

Remember never to pick wildflowers - they're an important part of our ecosystem, and pollinators need them more than you!

Grow Your Own Tomatoes

Tomatoes taste best picked straight off the vine. They love sunny weather and can be grown inside year-round or outside in the summer.

You will need:

- [ ] large yoghurt pots (washed and dried, with holes poked in the bottom for drainage) or small plant pots
- [ ] potting compost
- [ ] tomato seeds
- [ ] water
- [ ] trowel

How to grow:

1. Fill your yoghurt or plant pots with compost and tap them on a flat surface so the soil is level.

Potting Compost

tomato

2. Wet the compost with some tap water and let it drain. Gently press two or three tomato seeds into the pots, then cover with more compost.

3. Leave the pots on a warm, sunny windowsill to sprout.

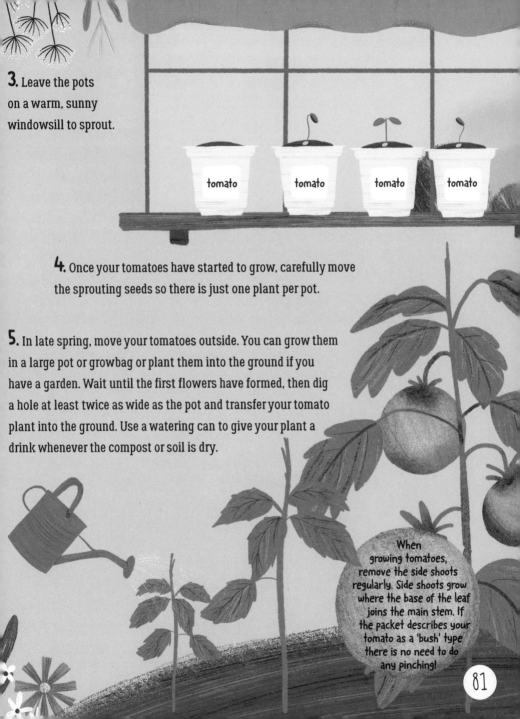

tomato   tomato   tomato   tomato

4. Once your tomatoes have started to grow, carefully move the sprouting seeds so there is just one plant per pot.

5. In late spring, move your tomatoes outside. You can grow them in a large pot or growbag or plant them into the ground if you have a garden. Wait until the first flowers have formed, then dig a hole at least twice as wide as the pot and transfer your tomato plant into the ground. Use a watering can to give your plant a drink whenever the compost or soil is dry.

When growing tomatoes, remove the side shoots regularly. Side shoots grow where the base of the leaf joins the main stem. If the packet describes your tomato as a 'bush' type there is no need to do any pinching!

81

Look Closer

Bee present

Take some time to examine the amazing miniature dramas unfolding in the garden.

1. On a calm, sunny day, find some flowers that are being visited by bees, hoverflies or butterflies.

2. Stand or sit in a comfortable position, and watch the flowers. When a pollinator comes to visit, give it your full attention. Note how it moves, the colour of its wings, its texture and any special markings. Can you see any yellow pollen on its body?

3. Listen out for any noises the insect might be making too. Do its wings hum as it flies, or fall silent when it lands?

Nature patterns

There are all kinds of interesting shapes and botanical patterns in nature. Some of the most special patterns are called fractals, which are geometrical shapes that repeat in bigger and smaller scales within the same structure. Some examples of fractals are ferns, snowflakes and snail shells. Studies have shown that the same areas of the brain that become active when listening to beautiful music, also become active when looking at fractals! How many can you spot, next time you're out and about?

Make a Nature Frame

Create a beautiful frame to display a wildlife photograph or nature drawing.

You will need:

- [ ] cardboard, or thick card
- [ ] pencil
- [ ] something to frame
- [ ] twine
- [ ] scissors
- [ ] sticky tac or tape
- [ ] pressed leaves and flowers (flick to page 48 to find out how to make these)

How to make:

1. Draw around the photo or drawing you want to frame on your piece of cardboard.

2. Cut out the shape you have drawn, making it a couple of millimetres smaller, so you'll be able to stick your picture behind without a gap.

3. Wrap twine around your frame, securing it at the back using sticky tape. Poke your pressed leaves and flowers between the twine, being careful not to damage them.

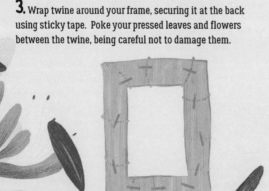

4. Stick your picture to the back of your frame using sticky tac or tape.

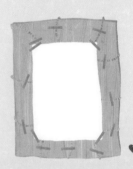

You can practise drawing on this page.

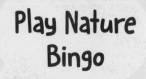

Play Nature Bingo

How to play:

Keep your eyes peeled for nature signs with this fun summer game.

1. One of the grids is for you, the other is for your friend. You might want to photocopy one of the grids, so your friend can carry their own.

2. While you walk around your garden or a local park, keep an eye out for the nature items on your cards. Mark them off as you spot them.

3. The aim is to be the first person to cross off a whole row. A row can be across, down or diagonal. Once you've completed a row, be sure to shout, "BINGO!"

4. You can carry on to see if you can spot all sixteen items on your cards. Shout "FULL GARDEN!" when you have crossed them all off.

You will need:

☐ a friend to play with
☐ two pencils

Your Nature Diary

Use these pages to jot down any interesting observations
you've made in the garden this year.

Glossary

bacteria   Tiny organisms that live on, in and around most living and non-living things. Some can be harmful and cause disease.

bark   The outer layer of a tree's trunk.

bloom   To produce a flower.

bulb   To produce a flower.

compost   A type of soil, good for growing plants in. Garden compost for adding to soil is made from a mixture of rotting matter, such as leaves, kitchen scraps and grass. Potting compost is good for growing pot plants in.

coniferous   Trees that produce cones – many keep their leaves all year round, such as pine trees and fir trees.

deciduous   Plants and trees that lose their leaves at certain times of the year, such as oak trees and maple trees.

decompose   To break down, decay and become rotten.

edible   Something that can be eaten.

evergreen   Plants and trees that keep their leaves all year round, such as holly and palms.

floret   A small flower, often one that makes up part of a bigger flowerhead.

flower   The part of a plant that blooms, has petals and makes fruits or seeds.

forage   To search for food.

germinate   When a seed begins to sprout.

germs   Very small organisms or bugs that often causes diseases.

harvest	Collecting seeds or picking fruits, vegetables or other edible plants.
herb	A plant which is used to flavour food.
hygiene	Anything you do to keep yourself and your surroundings clean and healthy.
nectar	A plant which is used to flavour food.
nocturnal animals	Creatures that are active at night and sleep during the day.
poisonous	Something that will make you ill or even kill you if you eat it.
pollen	Fine grains produced by the male parts of flowers that combine with the female parts of plants to produce seeds.
pollination	The process where pollen is moved from a male part to a female part of a plant, or between plants, so the plant can produce seeds.
pollinator	Animals and creatures that cause pollination to happen by transferring pollen, such as bees, bats and birds. Some plants are pollinated by the wind.
root	The part of the plant which gives it support by attaching it to the ground. The roots also carry water and nutrients from the soil to the rest of the plant.
seed	A small part of a plant from which new plants grow.
seedling	A young plant that has developed from a seed.
sow	To plant seeds.
stem	The stalk of a plant.
trowel	A small garden tool with a pointed scoop.
weed	A plant that gardeners want to pull up because it is pushing out its neighbouring plants or growing in the wrong place.

Index